Side Hustle Blueprint

How to Make an Extra $1000 in 30 Days Without Leaving Your Day Job!

2nd Edition

Lise Cartwright

Copyright © 2018 Lise Cartwright

All rights reserved. No part of this publication may be reproduced, distributed, or transmitted in any form or by any means, including photocopying, recording, or other electronic or mechanical methods, without the prior written permission of the publisher, except in the case of brief quotations embodied in reviews and certain other non-commercial uses permitted by copyright law.

ISBN-13: 978-1720616726

ISBN-10: 1720616728

For queries, please email: lise@hustleandgroove.com

www.hustleandgroove.com

READ FIRST:

As a massive thank you for investing in my book, I'd love to offer you instant access to the *Hustle & Grove Secret Vault of goodies + the SHB Workbook*.

Both will help you achieve success faster in your side hustle!

Visit this link to get started: http://www.hustleandgroove.com/shb-bonuses

Acknowledgements

There were so many people that inspired me to write this book, and there were also so many amazing people that helped refine my ideas and make this book come to life. Thank you for your support and for helping to make this book great!

Thanks in particular to Karen Marston and Harrison Tsai for helping me out and pushing me forward!

Table of Contents

Welcome 8
How This Guide Works 22
Step 1: The Idea 28
   Choosing Your Idea 28
   Step 1 - Action List 38
Step 2: Online Presence 40
   Online Profiles 40
   Your Website 46
   Step 2 - Action List 51
Step 3: Clients/Customers 52
   Finding Your Target Audience 52
   The Beginners Guide to Finding
Clients & Customers 59
   Step 3 - Action List 81
Step 4: Making The Sale 84
   Pitches & Proposals 84
   Product Pages 96
   Pricing and Rates 100
   Marketing 101 103
   Step 4 - Action List 112

Step 5: Contracts, Terms & Setup ___114

    Contracts 101 _____114

    Terms 101 _____119

    Managing Payments _____120

    Business Setup _____123

    Step 5 - Action List _____129

Step 6: Managing Time _____132

    Time Management _____132

    Step 6 - Action List _____142

What's Next _____144

Resources _____148

About the Author _____157

Urgent Plea _____158

More Books by the Author _____159

WELCOME

An Introduction

"I have more hustle in this finger than Skittles has candy." ~ Gary Vaynerchuk

Struggling to make ends meet? I feel your pain.

When was the last time you were able to buy yourself something special, pay off a bill in one go, or just buy yourself lunch?

I'm guessing it's been a while ... otherwise, why would you feel the need to pick up this book?

I get it. Life and all it encompasses can prevent you from getting the things you want and sometimes, the things you need.

Just when you get yourself back on track, something else always seems to pop up.

Things, like a bill that you hadn't accounted for, someone's birthday, a payment for that furniture you took deferred payments on... these can stop you from making ends meet and doing the things you want to do.

No wonder you're struggling— and savings, you don't even know when the last time was that you were able to save anything more than couple hundred dollars.

Picture this:
It's payday. It's also the end of the week— Wahoo! The weekend is here. You've been hanging out to get paid, so you can get the landlord off your back for being a week behind in rent. You've also earmarked some funds for Friday night drinks because, let's face it, you DESERVE it!

Your pay goes into your account, and, hey presto, all your outgoings take care of a good 80% of your pay. You're left wondering how you're going to make that 20% last until your next payday.

Does this scenario sound at all familiar?

Or maybe, this is more like you:

You've been working from home for the past two years. You're making more than you were in your full-time job, but you just can't seem to find any spare cash to save.

You feel like your outgoings aren't much more than when you were working for someone else. But for some reason, you're money skips right out the door the minute it hits your bank account.

Your 'payday' is not one set day of the week, so you struggle to budget everything and cash flow ... ha-ha, you laugh out loud— what is that?

If these scenarios sound at all familiar to you, then YOU know that money, no matter how great you are at budgeting, has a unique way of disappearing, often faster than you have time to tick things off the budget!

No matter your situation, we're all guilty of pushing aside what we should pay for and overspending on other things we don't need such as Friday night drinks, fast food, clothing and everything else in between.

We tell ourselves time and again, "I'll start a new budget tomorrow. I'll sit down and get this shit figured out," only to be in the same position come next payday.

With these types of struggles, it's easy to see why money and finances, in general, are one of the most popular topics discussed in new articles, websites, and books all the time.

The financial crisis, remember that? Some of us are still trying to dig ourselves out of that debacle!

And while you'll find plenty of books written on this subject, there will never be (or ever be) one book or program that answers every problem for every person because we're all unique and our situations are always different.

Yet, there is one book that provides solutions to your constant money struggles in ways that are easy to put in place and will make a real difference in your life right now.

And guess what? You've got it in your hot, little hands!

Side Hustle Blueprint: How to make an extra $1000 per month without leaving your day job has been developed to help you achieve a better lifestyle, allowing you to buy the things you want and pay for things when you need them.

It's delivered in a succinct and easy-to-read manner.

This book is for anyone who suffers from budget nightmares, lack of cash flow, and a profane loathing for credit cards, as well as annoying "I don't care about you" financial advisors.

As a previous full-time employee who developed a side income without leaving my job, I've mastered the art of creating income through my 'side hustles.'

I turned freelance writing into my full-time income after a short 10 months of working at it every day.

During this time, I read and tested a lot of different ideas, which lead me to the lifestyle I'm happy with right now.

Since I'm pretty sure you lack the time (and if we're being honest, the inclination) to do all the research and testing I've already done, I've compiled this book to provide YOU with the information you need to start your own side hustle(s).

You don't need to leave your day job (unless you want too!). You'll find all the information you need to get started, right here in this book.

Office workers, students, parents, creative entrepreneurs and many others who struggle with their finances and are trying to figure out ways to earn an extra dollar, have already experienced success by implementing and taking action.

They've read the information provided in this helpful how-to guide and taken action.

Jay, a full-time finance advisor in New York, said that after reading through the first step, he was ready to hit the ground running. *"Lise provided so many ideas that it sparked my own side hustle idea and I read the rest of the book in under 2 hours so I could get started right away!"*

Although this book is designed to help you make some extra cash and increase your side hustling skill set, these outcomes still need effort on your part. If you don't follow what's outlined in this book, nothing will change. It's that simple.

The ideas and steps outlined in this book provide a blueprint that can be implemented and actioned by anyone, anywhere, no matter what type of job the person has.

Take Leigh for example, she's a real estate agent in Australia, in her 50's and looking for a way to get out of this line of work. After reading *Side Hustle Blueprint*, she has set up her own freelance writing side hustle. *"I provide blog content and social media posts for other real estate agents. It really clicked for me when I saw the different types of side hustle's available and from there, I just added my own spin on it."*

Whether you're stuck working in an office, working from home, juggling multiple start-ups, or chasing the kids around the house, there is an idea in here that WILL work for you.

As you read on, you'll learn about the different types of side gigs available and which ones allow you to hit the ground running in the least amount of time.

I've spent the last 4 years working full-time as a freelance writer, self-published author and coach. I've tested loads of ideas, tips, and hacks to get myself to this point.

When I started out, I was working full-time for an employer with about 10 hours a week that I was prepared to set aside for my side hustle.

This allowed me to learn, through trial and error, about ways that I could make an extra income without having to leave my day job, so I could buy lunch whenever I wanted to and go for Friday drinks without trying to figure out where the money was going to come from.

This book is split into the steps you need to take to set up your side hustle.

You'll learn:

- Types of side hustle gigs you can use to make extra cash in the shortest amount of time
- Where to find clients and customers — because without them, your side hustle will fizzle into nothing as soon as you think of it

- What to include in a proposal when applying for different side gigs
- How to balance your side hustle with your job and busy lifestyle

In the words of Richard Branson, *"The best way of learning about anything is by doing."*

Side Hustle Blueprint: How to make an extra $1000 per month without leaving your day job provides you with clear and actionable steps to get started. You will make an extra $1000 per month in 30 days or less — if you follow the steps and take action.

This book is straight to the point (I don't beat around the bush.). It will help you achieve your financial goals much more quickly than if you were to continue as you have— struggling and just getting by.

I promise that if you follow the steps laid out in this book, you'll achieve an extra $1000 per month three times faster than if you just continued to do what you're doing now.

AND I promise that you'll achieve a more balanced financial outlook on life, where you can make decisions based on what you want and need, not based on how much something costs.

Who knows, you might enjoy your side hustle so much that you decide to make it your full-time gig, kicking that job of yours to the curb!

But, before you jump straight in, I'd like to share something with you that you should keep in the back of your mind while reading the book.

By following this one piece of advice, you put yourself in the top 10% of successful people (think Richard Branson!).

Failure to follow this one idea leads to unhealthy financial lifestyle habits, rather than making more income.

Are you ready for it? Here it is...

LEARN. DO. REPEAT.

If you want to be successful at anything in life, you have to take action.

Successful people excel over unsuccessful people because they understand the art of learning, doing and then repeating. They absorb and apply this learning quickly.

People who think outside the square and look beyond their current means of earning do so because they're looking for something more, to achieve financial freedom, to make a change in their life that provides more than they currently have access to.

They learn more quickly and implement what works immediately.

How many times have you thought to yourself, "I WISH I earned more. I WISH I had another way of making extra money without having to risk my job," only to stop there and never take any further steps to do something about it?

Don't be the person who sits and wishes they could do something about their financial situation but does nothing to make the change.

Be the kind of person that other people look to for

guidance; set an example by taking action.

Be the person that other people see and say, "I don't know how they can afford to eat out all the time AND pay the bills."

Be the kind of person who implements what is learned and who takes action quickly.

My final word is that the only people who shouldn't continue reading this book are those that already have everything they want financially.

They have savings in the bank, bills paid to date, and the ability to buy what they want, when they want. For the rest of us, there's always room to grow and change. If you're not happy with your finances, then you're in the right place.

The ideas presented in this book are proven to create life-changing results. All you have to do to access the things you want and need financially is to keep reading.

Each chapter will provide insights as you strive to find the right idea to help you make an extra $1000 per month, as quickly as possible.

Take control of your finances right now. Make them work for you, and create a lifestyle you love without all the extra stress of struggling to pay bills.

On the next few pages, you're going to learn how exactly to use this blueprint. Then it's straight to the heart of it— identifying the right idea or path that is going to lead you to the moola. Turn the page to get started!

HOW THIS GUIDE WORKS

How to Use This Book to Your Advantage

Before you read any further, make sure you grab the Side Hustle Blueprint PDF Workbook. Use it to record your ideas and thoughts as you work you way through each chapter. You can grab it here: http://www.hustleandgroove.com/shb-bonuses

Let's get something straight. This book will not give you an easy, instant method to make squillions of cash. What it will give you is the exact steps I took to make extra income, on the side, while working full-time.

I made $1000 in my first month just by using the steps I'm about to share with you.

The best way to make this guide work for you is to follow the steps in the order they appear. Jumping ahead means you'll skip out on learning key points.

If you feel that you already know something, I'd

still caution you about jumping ahead. But in the end, you know you, so I'll leave it up to you to make those decisions.

This is NOT a definitive guide. Each skill outlined in this book needs slightly different approaches when it comes to finding clients/customers and connecting with them. But the basic principles still apply, no matter what skill you decide to use as your side hustle.

Before we get started, let's address the questions you're likely to have at this point. It's best to get these out of the way, so you can start with a clear head and no niggling voices trying to tell you otherwise!

FAQ: STARTING A SIDE HUSTLE

Q: Do I need to know how to do the skills you're outlining as potential side gigs?

A: Yes and no. It depends— if you decide to make freelance writing or blogging your side hustle, that's pretty easy.

If you decide that you want to create websites and

that's not a skill you already have, the learning curve is greater, which delays your start time in terms of earning money.

I'll guide you on which is your best course of action, no matter whether you have a specific skill set or not.

Q: What about taxes?

A: I'll touch on this in Chapter 6, but you will need to declare any extra income you earn. It's best to speak with an accountant to ensure that you don't pay more taxes than you need to.

There are deductions that you can claim that reduce your taxes, so make sure you're taking advantage of these.

Q: How many hours do I need to set aside to make an extra $1000 per month?

A: This is quite a subjective question and relies on your ability to find and land clients/customers (which I'll address fully in Chapter 4).

You also need to be able to do the work that you're

going to get paid to do. I spent 10+ hours per week on my side hustle when I was working full-time.

My job was only 40 hours per week. I started work early and finished work around 4pm most days. This gave me a good couple of hours to work on my side hustle before my husband came home.

We also didn't have kids to worry about either.

It's about working with what you've got, prioritising the time you have.

Short-term pain for long-term gains.

I'll provide more advice about this as you work through the book.

Q: What if I only want to earn an additional $500 per month— will this guide help me?

A: Yes! It's up to you how much income you make in the end. You could definitely make an extra $500 per month working an extra 5 hours per week on top of your normal day job.

Q: Will I need to spend any money to get started on

my side hustle?

A: No. Everything that I outline in this book can be done for free. Where fees are applicable, I'll let you know. But for the most part, you can get yourself started without spending any money AT ALL.

If you have any further questions or feel that I haven't answered them in the book, please send an email to lise@hustleandgroove.com. I respond to all emails within 24 hours.

Now that we've cleared up any misgivings you might have, let's get started.

In the next chapter, we're going to focus on Step 1 in the process. You're going to find out exactly what types of skills you can access to make extra cash. Some of them are obvious, others not so much. Pick the one that provides the **lowest barrier to entry for you** and start! Turn the page to learn more.

STOP! Did you grab the PDF Workbook yet? You can grab it here: http://www.hustleandgroove.com/shb-bonuses

STEP 1: THE IDEA

Choosing Your Idea

"The Dream is free, but the hustle is sold separately."
~ Gary Vaynerchuk

You're probably excited to get to this step— after all, without this step, you can't move forward!

Take a bit of time deciding which avenue you're going to pursue to make sure that you give yourself the best shot at the side hustle you pick.

I know that sounds convoluted, but here's what you need to keep in mind when determining what skill you're going to focus on:

1. Is there a skill that you already have from the list below?
2. Which skill will allow you to get started as soon as possible?
3. If you do need some additional training, how long will this take?

If you keep these three thoughts in mind as we progress through this step, you'll ensure you're putting your best foot forward.

When it comes to choosing a side hustle, a lot of people think they don't have any skills available that they can further monetize outside of their normal jobs. I'm here to tell you that you do!

Below is a list of ideas to get you started, but it's by no means definitive! Anything, and I mean anything, can be turned into a side hustle; you just have to think outside the box.

For ease of reading, I'm sectioning them into headings, so just jump to an area that you have skills in or that you're interested in looking into further.

> ***Note***: *You can see this list inside your workbook, where you can highlight options and make notes.*

Writing
- Blog writer

- SEO articles
- Website content
- Resume writer
- Report writer
- Essay writer
- Podcast transcriber
- Ebook writer
- Ghost writer
- Proof reader
- Copy editor
- Content editor
- Magazine editor
- Copywriter
- Song writer
- About page writer
- Autoresponder writer
- Email writer
- Speech writer
- Press releases

Graphics
- Logo designer
- Banner image designer
- Ebook cover designer
- Facebook Header designer
- Twitter Header designer
- Cartoons

- Illustrator
- Kindle comic book creator
- Presentation designer (think PowerPoint!)
- Photographer
- Flyer designer
- Brochure designer
- Business card designer
- Landing page designer
- Facebook post designer

Programmer
- .Net coder
- C++ coder
- PHP coder
- App designer
- App coder
- Wordpress websites
- Wordpress plugins
- Joomla/Drupal programmer
- JavaScript coder
- Database creator/designer
- Software tester
- SaaS developer

Audio/Video
- Podcast editor
- YouTube video creator

- Animated videos
- Promo videos
- Ebook trailers
- Audio book narration
- Podcast voiceover (intro and outro)
- Sound effects
- Music intros and outros
- Music lessons (teach an instrument)
- Custom ringtones

Online Marketing
- Web analytics
- Search engine optimisation
- Blog mentions/commenting
- Forum posting
- Domain research
- Keyword research
- Social media manager
- Facebook ad manager
- Pinterest promotion manager
- Twitter list builder
- Twitter chats manager
- Bookmarking
- Link building
- Website analysis

Advertising

- Radio adverts
- Banner advertising (physical and online)
- Flyer management
- Newspaper adverts
- Direct mail outs

Business
- Event planner
- Program manager
- Project manager
- Brand strategy
- Consulting (your specific skill set)
- Business advice/planning
- Virtual assistant services
- Financial planning and advice
- Startup strategy
- Crowdfunding campaign manager
- Market research
- Legal consulting
- Accounting services

Other
- At-home hairdresser
- Beautician services
- Dog walker
- Pet carer
- Babysitter

- Tech support (computer help)
- Specific software support (think Excel, Word, Outlook, etc.)
- Cleaner
- Home shopper
- Personal shopper

Phew, I don't know about you, but those are a lot of ideas! If you can't find something in there to make some extra income, shoot me an email (lise@hustleandgroove.com), and I'll come up with 5 ideas just for you!

Once you've chosen your side hustle from the list above (or come up with your own), you need to think about those three questions I mentioned previously:

1. Is there a skill set that you already have from the list?
2. Which skill set will allow you to get started as soon as possible?
3. If you do need some additional training, how long will this take?

Once you've answered those three questions, you need to think about whether you need to upskill on the skill set.

If you already have the skill, would you benefit from any further training? If you don't have the skill, where will you get your training?

WHERE TO FIND TRAINING

If you decide that you want to up-skill or need to get trained in the area you want to do, there are a few places you can go to get that sorted quickly. This also depends on the skill set you've chosen.

Some ideas, such as an at-home hairdresser or legal consultant, require a bit of training and are not ideal options if you don't already hold the skills in the first place. Keep it simple, and try to stick with what you know.

You can find further training on sites like:

- Udemy.com — tons of free, discounted and cheap courses on anything under the sun
- Skillshare.com — similar to Udemy, you'll find even more course options here
- Helpouts by Google (helpouts.google.com) — this is a great way to learn how to do something very cheaply with someone

beaming into your home via a Google Hangout to teach you
- Guides.co — this is a great online community of free and paid guides that will teach you anything you want to know, and it is all self-paced learning
- Fiverr.com — while not normally a place to go to learn how to do something, there are people selling their courses on here, so if you're boot-strapping, this is a good place to go to check out and see what's available for what you want to learn

Before you take any further steps, let's do a gut check— how are you feeling right now? Overwhelmed? I understand. It's a lot of information to take in.

What I recommend you do right now is put down your Kindle or Kindle app (or paperback if you've got the paperback version) and take five. Let things sink in a little, and then return with a fresh mind.

Welcome back! Are you all set to continue? Rested, relaxed and ready to take in what you need to learn to make some extra income? Good, let's move on and set up your online profile.

BONUS: *Grab the first module from the Side Hustle Blueprint Masterclass. It will walk you through exactly how to choose your side hustle skill or idea and which one to choose that will see you earning extra cash in the next 30 days.*

Grab it here:
http://www.hustleandgroove.com/qmgx

Step 1 - Action List

At the end of each step, you're going to find a quick check list of things to do. Ideally, you should aim to to complete these steps BEFORE you move onto the next step, however, you know you best, so do what works best for you.

:: Checklist

- Choose your side hustle idea (2-3 ideas initially)
- Do you need extra training? Start that now

Ready to move on? Congratulations! You've come far and achieved some great things.

The next few steps are going to blow your mind, so grab a cup of coffee and some pen and paper, and let's get cracking! Turn the page to learn all about setting up your online presence.

STEP 2: ONLINE PRESENCE

Online Profiles

The next thing you need to do is to set up your online presence the right way. It's time to put pen to paper or finger to keyboard, as the case may be.

Your online presence isn't just one site. Below is a list of the sites that I'm going to focus on in this section.

You don't have to do all of them, but I'd recommend you consider most of them. The more your name is out there, the more avenues for potential clients to find and connect with you.

- LinkedIn
- Twitter
- Facebook
- Pinterest
- Instagram

Let's start looking at your online presence.

LinkedIn

LinkedIn is often an under-utilized site when it comes to side hustling. It's for this reason that it's important that you have a good profile. Your potential clients are more likely to look here first than anywhere else online.

Don't worry. If you don't have a LinkedIn profile or can't set one up or adjust it because of the reasons outlined above, you have other options. I'll go into these later in this section.

For now, you want to ensure that your current LinkedIn profile is setup and optimized. If you want to keep your side hustle separate from your 'normal' LinkedIn profile, just set up a new one, making sure you use a different email address.

The reason I'm mentioning LinkedIn now is because this is where most potential clients do their own networking, so it makes sense that they would use LinkedIn to also look for potential people to work with as well.

You need to ensure that your LinkedIn profile is 100% complete. Make sure your profile reflects your experience and showcases the work you've completed.

If you don't have much experience in the skill your looking to make some extra income with, either skip LinkedIn or figure out a way to include your current skills in a way that highlights how these fit with your side hustle.

Make sure your summary has something compelling written in it, something that will make people want to read more about you.

You could rewrite the information from your overview/bio area on your resume or other social media profiles here. Here is my LinkedIn profile (nz.linkedin.com/in/lisecartwright/) for your reference, so you get a clear idea of what I mean.

The last word on LinkedIn is that you need to ensure you have a good, clear profile image.

Where possible, try and make sure you use the same image across all of your online profiles, whether that's your Facebook page or Twitter profile. It helps develop your brand (which is YOU) and makes you more recognizable to potential clients.

Twitter
With Twitter, you want to make sure you've included a link to your personal website (if you have one) or another site that clearly lets people know who you are and how they can contact you. If you don't have a personal website, link back to your LinkedIn profile.

Make sure that your profile image is clear and either the same as your LinkedIn profile image or similar. Make your header image something meaningful such as the name for your side hustle or even just your name.

Use sites like Canva.com to create this for you. You can use their Twitter header template to come up with something unique and eye-catching if you don't have this set up.

You can view my Twitter profile (www.twitter.com/Lisecnz) to get an idea of what this looks like.

Facebook
A word of caution about using Facebook to connect with potential clients. Don't provide them a link or

add them as a friend if you've got a lot of drunken photos on your profile!

Instead, create a page (resource: https://www.facebook.com/help/104002523024878) that is dedicated to your new side hustle. You don't have to spend a lot of time setting this up. It's just another way for potential clients to connect with you and learn what it is you do. You're providing a personal touch.

You can use Canva.com to setup your Facebook Page header image as well. Make sure you use the profile image that you've already used on your other profiles.

Fill in as much detail as possible and make sure that you're sharing content on this page at least once a day. Make it related to your side gig or what potential clients might like to know about you or the service you're offering.

Pinterest
As with Twitter, you want to make sure you include a link to your personal website in your Pinterest profile, as well as a little about what it is you do or provide. You can see my Pinterest profile here:

http://www.pinterest.com/lisecnz

You can start with a personal account if you want, but if you're serious about your side hustle, then consider switching to a business account — it costs nothing to do this, so why not?

You'll get extra benefits by being able to see your analytics, which will be helpful further down the track.

If you have a product-based side hustle, then Pinterest is definitely a platform you should be on. Hello, visuals anyone?!

Instagram
Include a brief bio about what is you do and who you help.

Include a link to your website as well, make it easy for potential clients or customers to find you.

Try and keep your images similar, i.e., similar colors, similar filters used and if you're open to video, try out Instastories as well.

If you want to see how my Instagram looks, you'll

find me under @lisecnz.

Your Website

About.me

About.me is a great resource to use as your about page if you want to keep your other profiles separate from your side hustle. This is a free service and allows you to connect with potential clients in a professional manner.

Choose your background image carefully. You could use an image of yourself or go with a landscape or logo image. It's up to you.

About.me is a more modern version of LinkedIn, and if you want to keep your boss from finding out what you're up to in your spare time, this is the site I'd recommend you setup.

Choose your URL (i.e., about.me/yourname) wisely. If you don't want people to find you by your name, choose something else, like a pen name. You can view my about me page (http://about.me/lisecartwright) for an idea of what's included and shown.

This is also a good alternative as your personal

website if you don't want the hassle of paying for hosting.

The pro version allows you to have a custom domain name too.

Otherwise, a personal website is your next option.

Personal Website
Some of you may already have a personal website or blog set up which you may choose to use, or you can create something new. At the least, you should have a website or about.me site over the online profiles listed above.

What I mean by this is that your own website or about.me page is more important than having all these online profiles. Either will provide you with a good business front and then you can add the other profiles further down the track if you want to.

There are several reasons why your website is better than other online profiles:

1. It provides you with the ability to showcase your skills through a portfolio, whether that's showing off your design skills, writing

skills, or hairdressing skills. You have the option to do this by using images, words, video and audio. Basically any digital medium you can think of can be used to show off what you can do.
2. It provides a professional image to any potential clients. It looks great when you send a potential client to your site, and they can see that you're a real person.
3. It allows you to promote your services. The site is all about you, so you needn't worry about coming off as all 'salesy' because it's your site!

If you're looking to get yourself up and running quickly and don't want to spend a lot of money setting something up, here are some sites to consider:

- Wix.com— you can set up a great website in under an hour without having to spend a dime on hosting or domain name registration
- Weebly.com— the same as Wix, no money required to get yourself up and running
- Portfoliobox.net— if your skill set is more on the creative side, this type of website

- Crevado.com— another alternative for your creative skills
- Wordpress.com— use this if you think you'll turn your side gig into a full-time thing, as it can easily morph into a hosted website with your own domain name at the press of a few buttons
- Wordpress.org — use this if you want a self-hosted website and custom theme with email marketing options

With the pages on your website, at the bare minimum, include an about page (like your about.me profile), a portfolio page that showcases your work (create some examples if you haven't done any yet), a landing page that talks about what you do and a contact page so people can reach you via email.

You can see an example here: www.writearticlesnow.com

As a bonus and if you have the time, I'd also recommend adding a blog to your site. Only do this if you can publish weekly on the blog. If you're looking at any of the writing ideas, this is a must-have.

A blog will not only serve as an extra space to showcase your writing skills, but it will also improve your writing.

You can see a blog in action by visiting my blog at www.hustleandgroove.com.

This is a self-hosted Wordpress.org site with OptimizePress2 as the theme.

Ok, that's enough for Step 2!

Step 2 - Action List

At the end of each step, you're going to find a quick check list of things to do. Ideally, you should aim to to complete these steps BEFORE you move onto the next step, however, you know you best, so do what works best for you.

:: Checklist

- Setup your online profiles, ensuring they are properly optimised
- Setup your website (see the resource page for more on how to do this)

You want to put your best foot forward and make sure that potential clients get the right first impression. Make sure this is all set up before moving to Step 3.

Ready to move on? Congratulations! You've come far and achieved some great things. The next few steps are going to blow your mind, so grab a cup of coffee and some pen and paper, and let's get cracking!

Turn the page to learn how to find your first client.

STEP 3: CLIENTS/CUSTOMERS

Finding Your Target Audience

"If someone offers you an amazing opportunity and you're not sure you can do it, say yes - then learn how to do it later." ~ Richard Branson

Before we delve in too much further, let's address that nagging thought in the back of your mind, the one about your boss or company finding out about what you're doing.

Depending on where you work and your company's policy around taking on extra work, this could be a real concern for you.

Luckily for me, when I started doing my side hustle, my company never found out about it, and it never interfered with my work, so they never had any cause to investigate why I wasn't meeting deadlines (because I WAS!).

So let's do another gut check here and consider your options:

CHECK YOUR CONTRACTS

Have you checked your contract? Is there anything in there that prohibits you from taking on additional work in your spare time? - Nothing? Full speed ahead! - Something? Refer to the next point...

Can you talk to your boss? Are you able to have an open conversation with your boss and ask for permission to do a little extra work on the side? This works best if the type of service you're looking to provide is NOT directly related to your immediate job. Yes, arrange the meeting! If you don't feel comfortable or it's just a no-fly zone, move to the next point.

How badly do you need the extra income? Are you prepared to work under a pen name or pseudonym instead? This is your best option if the other two options aren't available or doable. If this is your only option, then don't worry about setting up a LinkedIn account or Facebook account (or linking to them).

FINDING YOUR AUDIENCE

This was one of the areas I struggled with initially

when I first started. Sure, it was easy to figure out what I wanted to do as my side hustle, but to actually turn that into a skill where clients would pay me for it —overwhelming! I had no idea where to start.

Now that I do, I'm here to pass on to you what you need to do to find your first few clients or customers.

Finding clients and customers is the cornerstone of any successful business. Whether you're freelancing to make a bit of extra income or running a full-time business, without clients and customers, you won't make any money.

It can be daunting trying to find clients and customers, particularly if you've never had to do this as part of your normal day job.

I remember thinking when I first started, that all I had to do was get my online presence set up and wait for the flurry of client requests that would flood my inbox.

I wasn't familiar with online marketing, and I thought that Google would start promoting my website to thousands of potential clients just because I had a brand new website up and running ... cue crickets chirping here!

Talk about naive, right?

Needless to say, it was a slow first month in my side hustle, until someone said to me, "Lise, what are you DOING to promote your services?"

"Um, doesn't Google take care of that?"

I won't relay the response I got to this, but let's just say there was a LOT of laughter and plenty of finger pointing.

This step is the most important part of the process, but it's not the only area to focus on.

Make sure you've completed **Step 1** before you embark down the path of finding clients and customers.

Sure, you can wing a lot of things in the beginning, I definitely did, but if you want to put your best foot forward, make sure you've ticked off the following items:

- ✓ You have your website or some sort of online presence completed
- ✓ You have some portfolio items on your site (create them if you don't have any)
- ✓ Your site shows a way for clients to contact you
- ✓ You have at least two social media profiles setup (I'd recommend Twitter and LinkedIn/Facebook at minimum)
- ✓ You have Skype or Google Hangouts operational

Ok, now that we've got that covered, let's find your target audience!

Now, I'm not going to bore you with a whole bunch of marketing speak here.

I'm not even going to get you to do one those buyer persona thingee's, because quite frankly, they are a little intimidating.

Instead, do the following exercises:

#1: What problem does your product or service solve?

Write down the answer to this question. It could be as simple as providing custom content that saves clients time and increases engagement.

This would be something you might write if you were a blogger or copywriter.

If you have a product, say a clutch purse, then you might write something like:

I provide beautiful, handmade clutch purses that protect your precious items from harm, while also looking fashionable.

Be very specific about the problem your solving from your client or customers point of view.

#2: Who is your ideal client or customer?

I want you to paint a picture... think of a person (maybe someone you know) that might be your ideal client or customer.

You need this image in your mind so you know who you're 'talking' to when you start creating marketing information.

So think about things like:

- Age
- Gender
- Income
- Marital status
- What do they like to do in spare time?

#3: Create your target audience 'definition'

Now I know that might sound intimidating, but all it does is helps you come up with a one-word sentence to focus on as we move forward.

Here's the formula for it:

"[INSERT YOUR NAME] creates/provides [PRODUCT OR SERVICE] to help [INSERT DEMOGRAPHIC] so they can [INSERT WHAT SOLVES PROBLEM] better."

This is what it might look like if you were a copywriter working with mompreneurs:

"Julie Smith creates engaging copywriting to help time-poor mompreneurs so they can spend more time with their children and focus on their business better".

And if you were that cloth purse designer, here's what it might look like for you:

"Kim Thomas creates beautiful, hand-made clutches to help fashion-conscious women protect their precious items and look great during any event."

Spend a bit of time on getting this just right, as it will help you throughout the rest of this book.

In the next section, we're going to focus on how to find those ideal clients or customers.

The Beginners Guide to Finding Clients & Customers

Depending on the product or service you're providing, there are some obvious places to start.

If the product or service you're providing is something that you've been doing/had for a while, it makes sense to reach out to your immediate network.

Think friends and family here, not your co-workers or close clients, definitely a no-no, particularly if you want to keep your workplace in the dark about what you're doing!

For now, you want to keep your day job and your side hustle separate. Use your network, but be smart about whom you're approaching.

If your side hustle is something new that you've just learned or have been doing as a hobby for a while, you can still tap into your network, but the approach you use will be different.

Tap Into Your Network

1. If your network is familiar with your product or service because it's something you were doing (or are doing) in your day job, then a simple email, message on LinkedIn or direct message on Twitter is a good way to go. A simple announcement letting them know what you're offering and that you're providing a 25% discount (or similar) for first-time users of your service

should garner you a few clients fairly quickly.
2. If your network is not familiar with the service you're looking to provide, still chat with them, but offer to do your service for free for the first 5 people that get in touch with you. By doing this, you build your credibility, and you will have some real-world items to add to your portfolio!
3. Another option you might not have considered is to check your smartphone. You may have contacts there that you've likely forgotten about. Make sure you check your phone as well to ensure you're hitting these people too. Don't be spammy though - if you don't 'know' someone, then don't contact him or her.

Your network is full of people who are your biggest advocates. They are the people who will help you get something going if you reach out and ask. If you don't ask, nothing will happen and you'll be like I was, listening to crickets ...!

Service-Based Side Hustles

Use Job Boards

This is my favourite place to start, outside of your network. It's also your best place to start if you don't want to tap into your existing network.

Job boards are excellent for specific side hustles and are a great way to find people who are looking for your specific skill set.

This is how I got started finding clients. I used oDesk (now Upwork) to find clients and make my first $1 as a freelance writer. Actually, I made $1000 with my first client on oDesk.

I'll let that sink in... When I started thinking about doing something on the side to increase my income, oDesk was one of the first sites that came up in my Google search, which is the main reason I went for it.

I had no previous knowledge of oDesk or what to expect, so I just jumped in and got started with completing my profile and applying for jobs.

In the section below, you'll learn how to 'pimp' out

your profile on sites like Upwork and how to write a proposal that gets you an interview. But for now, just focus on deciding where you'll look for your first few clients.

While Upwork is not the marketplace it used to be, it's a great place to get started, particularly if the service you're providing is a newly developed skill set.

Here's a list of some good places to start as a service-based side hustler:

- Craigslist.com— this is a good place to find people locally that you don't know. Use this option if you're providing services like writing or hairdressing. In fact, you'll probably find at least one job here no matter what service you provide
- Freelancer.com— similar to Upwork, you need to have a complete profile, and it may cost you a subscription fee to access specific jobs
- Dice.com— if you're side hustle is tech related, this is a good option for you to start
- Problogger.net— any type of writing gig can be found on the job board at Problogger

with a focus on blogging and copywriting
- Smashing Jobs (jobs.smashingmagazine.com/) — designers and programmers will have the most success on this job site
- WeWorkRemotely.com — if you're not quite ready to enter freelancing, there are some remote job options here, a good stepping stone if you just want to test the waters and leave your current job for more flexibility
- HireWriters.com — any writing gig can be found here, cheap but a good way to build your portfolio
- AuthenticJobs.com — lots of different options here, both freelancing, moonlighting, and if you want a career change, there are also full-time options available

This is by no means a definitive list, but it's a great place to start. A job board is a really helpful place to find clients. It's a way for you to build a client base and kick-start what could lead to a full-time career change!

Setting up Your Profiles the Right Way
Before you move on, we need to make sure that

you set up profiles on sites like Upwork, Freelancer, Hire Writers, etc., the right way.

You may have already joined these sites. If you have, what does your profile say about you?

Does it say, "I'm experienced. Working with me is guaranteed to improve your bottom line," or does it say, "I'm new, not too sure what to tell you, but I want to work with you!"?

Who would you hire?

I've been working with these types of sites for over 4 years now, and there are definitely some key areas that you need to focus on.

**Resource: www.hustleandgroove.com/anatomy-of-an-awesome-odesk-profile

This is what you should focus on:

1. Your Photo. Your profile should have a good headshot image of you. If you don't have a photo on your profile, do this now. Keep it semi-professional, nice and clear. If you have a baby face— and I'm talking to you

gentleman out there— add a bit of facial hair, either through using Photoshop or growing some! A peer of mine did this and saw an increase from 12% to 35% in employer replies. You can see the full details about how he did this here (www.quora.com/oDesk/What-are-some-of-the-top-oDesk-hacks). If you're not comfortable with using your image, use your logo instead, but use something that makes sense to whatever side hustle you're promoting.

2. Your Overview/Bio Area. This is where most people make a huge mistake. They focus more on what they have achieved in their 'normal' day job, which does nothing to compel a potential client to want to work with them. Avoid making this mistake; write your overview/bio as if it were a sales letter. Think about what the client is looking for; tell them how you will meet their needs, their requirements. Including a money-back guarantee here is also a great way to cut the risk of working with you. Use headings to highlight key areas, and tell them what they can expect when they work with you. To see how your overview area should look in

practice, check out my Upwork profile here: http://www.upwork.com/o/profiles/users/_~01095282677fac80f4/

3. Complete Your Profile. This is also a common mistake many people make. A 100% complete profile ensures that you don't miss out on landing clients. This includes ensuring you have work listed in your portfolio and that you've completed your skills area. Taking some tests will also boost your profile, as it shows that you're qualified to do what you say you can. At least 7 tests is a good place to start.

Let's look at these areas closely:

Photo

In relation to your photo, you want to make sure it's a professional photo of you. Head and shoulders work best.

As I said, if you're not comfortable providing an image of yourself, make sure you use something that portrays your business such as a logo.

The aim is to make a personal connection with a potential client, which is a little hard to do if you don't have an image there. They are looking to make sure you're a real person and a professional. Make your photo count; make this the same image you've used on other profiles to establish brand consistency.

Overview/Bio
This is the most important aspect of your online profile on these sites. You should view this as a sales page and make the focus more on what you can do for the client, rather than talking all about you.

Aim to hit all the points that matter most to your client: what they will get working with you, what you're delivery times are, do you have a refund policy, etc.

Resume
In this area, you'll be able to upload your resume, but you'll also have the opportunity to manually fill in some of these details as well. Highlight any skills and talents you have that relate to your side hustle. Your actual resume should not be pages and pages long. Short and sweet works best; in fact, a one-page resume is ideal.

You can pick up my suggested template in the **Tips and Tools Guide Resources Page** here: http://www.hustleandgroove.com/shbresources16.

Portfolio

Use this area to showcase your work. If you haven't done any previous work (because this is a new skill), then create 3 to 5 items to add to your portfolio.

There are two ways that you can approach this:

1. Create some random items and upload them
2. Offer to do a couple of free jobs for family and friends

Tests

Depending on the site, you might be required to complete some tests as they relate to your side hustle. The more tests you complete, the better. Always complete tests that relate to your side hustle skill base and make sure that you only display (on your profile) those that you have passed. Hide any that you fail, and redo them when applicable.

The bottom line: If you've got an incomplete profile, one that doesn't outline what a client gets when working with you or doesn't show with examples (portfolio + tests) that you can do the skills you've listed, the likelihood of getting hired diminishes significantly.

Cold Emailing

A lot of people freak out when they think about cold emailing. And I understand why! It kinda of reminds me of those horrible tele-marketing companies calling right around dinner time, trying to sell you some timeshare apartment.

Well, I'm not talking about that type of cold email strategy.

The best thing about cold emailing is that it doesn't cost you anything and you can do it in conjunction with any of the other activities outlined in this chapter.

The key to a successful cold email strategy is in being able to stand out from all the other hundred's of emails that your potential client receives each day.

Here're are some tips on how to make cold emailing a little easier:

- Focus on a attention-grabbing subject line. It should be creative and relevant to the person reading it. This means no bulk emails — yuck! A great subject line is intriguing and makes them want to know what's inside. Try something like this: "Your social media marketing game plan" or "Um, are we gonna gel?"
- Get a professional email signature. You can do this easily on your Gmail account by using sites like <u>Wisestamp.com</u> or even your <u>about.me</u> page. Make sure it has all the relevant details and a link to your portfolio, product and/or website.
- Add a connection. The key to a successful cold email is finding a way to introduce some type of connection between you and your potential client. The way to do this is to take the time to find out their interests... Find something that you've got a shared interest in and mention it in your email. An example would be if you're located in the same city or like the same sports team.

They key with a cold email is to not make it generic. Take the time to do a bit of research about who you're reaching out to and you'll find you'll get better responses and you won't feel like one of those nasty tele-marketers.

Product-Based Side Hustles

Online Shopping Platforms
Using an online shopping platform to find more customers is a great way to kick-start your product-based side hustle.

Maybe you're selling custom designed t-shirts or hand-made coin purses.

Whatever your side hustle is, if it's product-based, setting up a profile on an online shopping platform makes complete sense.

Here're a few places you should checkout:

- <u>Etsy</u> — this is probably my favorite out of the online shopping platforms. Kind of like Amazon but for handmade products. It's free to get setup, but make sure you read about the charges and adjust your pricing

accordingly.
- eBay — I'm sure you've heard of this one already. A huge marketplace that gives you the option to go global. Include a link back to your main website as well if you want to capture email addresses.
- Shopify — while this isn't necessarily the same as the two above, you do get a lot of the same features with the added bonus of this being an actual website rather than being hosted on a platform. This platform will cost you at least $30 per month, so if you're just getting started, maybe Etsy is a better option.
- Bonanza — very similar to Etsy, this site is one of the easiest to get set up on. Lower fees will have you enjoying utilizing this site.

Again, this isn't a definitive list, but it is a place to get started. These are definitely the top four most popular options, which means you'll have a ready-made audience there.

Make sure that you include a link to your main website within your profiles and any product listings you have, so that you're getting the benefit of traffic to your website, where you're (hopefully) capturing people's email addresses for ongoing marketing.

In the next section, I'm going to provide you with some different ways you can use your social media profiles to connect with your target audience.

Social Media is a great and easy way to reach out to potential clients and customers and is often overlooked.

Social Media Tips

This is probably one of the most under utilized ways to find clients or customers.
Most people know they need to have some sort of social media presence, but how many people do you know who have actively found a new job (or clients/customers) using social media?
There are a number of different ways that you can find your target audience using social media.

Start by choosing a couple of social media platforms, and use the following ideas to find your audience and start your side hustle.

#1: Network using social media

Connect with others that are in the same service as you or have a similar product, and chat with them on a regular basis.

The same 'old school' networking rules apply here: provide value, answer questions and don't spam.

Twitter is by far the best channel to do this on. A lot of side hustlers find clients via this social media channel simply through engaging with the people they follow, answering questions and joining in on industry chats.

Make sure your Twitter profile tells people what it is you do, links to your website, and start interacting now.

Another option with Twitter is to build lists of potential clients and customers (based on your target audience definition) and follow them, so you can monitor what they talk about.

A lot of people will reach out to their Twitter followers when they are looking for a specific skill or product.

#2: Let people know what you're working on

Social media is all about sharing, so why not share a current project you're working on if applicable?

As a side hustler, this works well in your favor. You can tweet about a topic you're working on, and if you're connected to some potential clients or customers, you'll be surprised at how often you'll get a comment or direct message about how they are looking for something similar or would like you to pitch your proposal to them.

#3: Increase credibility through content curation
(Definition: en.wikipedia.org/wiki/Content_curation)

When it comes to your public social media profiles, the focus shouldn't just be all about your own projects and links. You should also be sharing information from others in your industry.

Talk about your industry in an intelligent way, and people will remember that you know what you're talking about.

The key to doing this well is to be consistent with the topics you cover. This will only help to build your credibility and expert 'voice.'

#4: Brush up your LinkedIn profile

Like Twitter, LinkedIn has a much more business focus than many of the other social media platforms available.

As I've already said, only use LinkedIn if you're comfortable doing so. It's not a place where you'd put up an update about what you did on the weekend. Make sure you remember that when you're sharing via this platform.

Many businesses use LinkedIn as their go-to resource for locating people to work with, so make sure your profile is littered with keywords that are relevant to your side hustle.

A quick tip for mastering LinkedIn networking is to keep an eye on the 'who's viewed my profile' widget on the right-hand side of your profile or news feed.

Reach out to them via LinkedIn's internal email system, and drop them a quick note, something along the lines of:

Subject line: Were you looking for a freelance writer?

Hi [name]. I see you recently viewed my profile. If you're in need of a writer, I have experience in [your industry/niche]. I'd be happy to send you samples or chat more about what you need. Let me know if I can help!

[your signature]

This is a much better way than cold emailing!

#5: Join social media groups

Another way that you could use social media to find clients or customers is to take part in groups.

LinkedIn has a lot of groups that you can join, as does Facebook; on Twitter, you can join in on Twitter chats.

Pinterest has group boards, which is a great way to expand your reach as well.

Social media can be a great way to reach out to those people who are in your broader network, people that you may not personally know but are connected to you in some way.

By now, you should have a fairly good idea of where to find your ideal client or customer.

My advice to you is to start with your network. If that's not an option, then use sites like Upwork and Freelancer or Etsy to find your first few clients or customers, and then branch out to specific job boards or shopping platforms and your social media networks.

You'll also find that once you've landed a few clients or customers, you'll start to get referrals, and that's when things can start to get interesting.

You might start considering an exit strategy for leaving your full-time job at this point!

Spend 3 to 5 hours setting up your profile on sites like Upwork, Freelancer and Etsy as well as brushing up your social media profiles, or contact your network if that's the option you choose.

The aim is to apply for two jobs or connect with potential clients and customers, daily.

If you want to make an extra $1000 per month, then you need gigs or sales to do this. Land five gigs in a month, and you can definitely achieve this.

When I first started, I scheduled 30 minutes each day to find jobs on Upwork that I could apply for. I had a proposal template that I used and modified for each job and just applied to as many jobs as I could.

You should do the same. Treat this as a serious task, and you'll get serious results.

Step 3 - Action List

Remember, this checklist is here to ensure that you don't forget anything and that you follow the process. If you get stuck, circle back to the last step.

:: Checklist

- Read your company policy on taking on additional work outside of your job - do what you need to do!
- Identify your target audience using the exercises provided
- Connect with your network and let them know what you're up to (if applicable)
- Join job boards and set up profiles the right way
- Join Etsy or start a Shopify store for your product-based side hustle
- Utilise LinkedIn, Pinterest and Twitter to connect with clients/customers

In the next chapter, I'm going to share with you how to pitch clients the right way. We'll look at what you should include in your proposal and how you can ensure to at least land an interview.

You'll also learn how to set up your product pages the right way if you're selling a product, as well as how to price your product or service.

Let's jump straight to it.

STEP 4: MAKING THE SALE

Pitches & Proposals

For Service-Based Side Hustles

"There is no try. There is only do or do not." ~ Yoda

In this section, we're going to focus on how to best pitch a client and what to include in a proposal.

Because if you don't get this right, no matter how many gigs you apply for, all you'll get in response is ... crickets. (again, cue chirping noise!)

I don't think I have to say this, but I will. If you can't write a strong proposal or pitch, it's going to be difficult to land a gig with a client, no matter how great your profile or website is.

The art of communicating with clients online requires the ability to communicate well while also getting across what you will provide to a client in less than two pages.

If you disagree with what I've just said, then I think you need to stop right here, rewind and maybe give yourself a bit of a slap!

HELLO - if you can't effectively articulate in your proposal or pitch why a client would benefit working with you, how will you make any extra income and be successful in your new side hustle?

Um, you won't; it's that simple.

Now, before you stress out, I'm going to provide you with some tips on how to write a great pitch or proposal. I'll also provide you access to some proposals I've written and a template for you to use going forward.

When writing your proposal or pitch, you want to grab a potential client's attention fast.

Here's how you can do that:

1. Be straight to the point - tell them what you're applying for (clarify the position using their words.).
2. Use bullet points - list your qualifications

and experience in a bullet list. Just provide them the highlights as they relate to the job. They can learn more about you by viewing your profile or website.
3. Answer any questions - whether directly asked or implied. Make sure you understand the job, and answer any questions they ask. Failure to do this will result in your landing in the 'no' pile.

Use headings to separate your information. You want your proposal to be easy to skim and digest. If the client needs to know more info or delve deeper, they'll do this by looking at your online profiles and/or website.

These are some of the headings you should include:

- Experience/Qualifications
- What to Expect
- What's Next

Make sure you explain how the client can get in touch with you, and sign off appropriately.

Below is an example of a proposal I sent to a client.

You can access a similar template in the **Tips and Tools Resource Guide**.

Hi xx

Thanks for the opportunity to submit my proposal for this SEO Online Strategy position.

My Experience/Qualifications
I am an experienced online marketing professional, with over 5+ years experience, so I understand what is needed to help improve a sites SEO rankings.

A lot of this experience is in the local market within Australia, as well as internationally.

I manage my own site and that of several clients, utilizing social media and SEO strategies to get to the first page of Google in a legitimate, white-hat way.

My Proposal
As outlined in your job, I will provide the following:
- *Get your site to the first page of Google using legitimate SEO methods and sustain this position*
- *Provide statistics to track conversion rates*

- *Provide a 12-month strategy for online marketing*
- *Create high quality backlinks which are relevant to your site*

Next Steps

I am available to commence immediately and look forward to talking further about this position. I can be available for a Skype call should you wish to 'meet' face to face.

Attached with this proposal is my resume, outlining my experience in detail as well as testimonials from previous clients and a link to my portfolio.

I look forward to hearing from you soon.

Your name

Make sure that you always attach your one-page resume (or online resume - http://www.hustleandgroove.com/online-resume) and link to your portfolio items, either through your online profile (if applying via Upwork, Freelancer or Etsy) or your website.

The above is what you should include in a proposal

when applying via a job board or outsourcing site.

If you're applying via email, i.e., a direct contact, then your pitch will be a little different.

Refer to the cold emailing section in the previous chapter as well.

An email pitch consists of 3 different sections:

1. Cover letter
2. Proposal
3. Resume

In an online proposal pitch, your cover letter and proposal are the same thing. But when applying via email, you need to go that extra step to grab the client's attention.

Let's start with the cover letter:

- Use a professional and friendly greeting. If possible, greet the person by first name (if you know it).
- Outline what you're applying for, how you found the job and how you understand the job folding out. If you're cold pitching,

outline why you think they need your services and include testimonials and/or case studies to illustrate how good you are and how you can help them
- Use a bulleted list to highlight your experience and qualifications, and also list what you've included as attachments to the email.
- Sign off, making sure that all your contact information is in your email signature.

Once you've nailed the cover letter, outline your proposal much the same way, but be sure to provide a bit more detail in what the client can expect when working with you as well as any other details they might need, such as a link to your portfolio.

Your resume should highlight the relevant skill set for this position and should definitely be one page.

Short and to-the-point is key here. It shows you respect their time.

Make sure all your contact information is included in your resume as well. Include your Skype ID to make it as easy as possible for a client to reach you.

You can find the email template that I use to pitch clients in the **Tips and Tools Resource Guide**.

Once you've sent your proposal or pitch, you should be available for an interview over the next few days. Watch your email for your client's response!

Interviewing can be nerve-racking the first time around which is why I've prepared some tips on how to make sure you ace your interview.

On the next page, you'll learn how you can nail your interview the first time around, what questions you should ask and when to ask for more details. Read on to learn more.

Nailing Your Interview

If possible, you'll want the interview to take place via Skype. Some clients may wish to video chat with you, but most will just stick with calling you.

If they are local, they may want to meet in person, so be prepared for this too.

Make sure that you have Skype set up correctly and

that the audio and video work.

Here's how to set up your Skype: www.wikihow.com/Set-up-a-Skype-Account.

Once you've confirmed that your system is all set up you can move on to focusing on your interviewing skills.

Follow these tips to ensure you nail your interview:

1. Always dress professionally - regardless of whether this will be an audio or video chat. How you dress influences how you come across. Give yourself the best opportunity by dressing like you would for a 'normal' job interview.
2. If you're doing the call via audio only, stand up during the call. Don't stay seated. This allows you to stay focused, and you'll feel more confident. It also allows you to punctuate what you say with body movements, which come through well over audio.
3. Smile during the interview, regardless of whether they can see you or not. It will

come through in your voice and adds to your personality.
4. Listen! Wait until the client finishes speaking before replying. Talking over a potential client NEVER turns out well.
5. Come prepared with questions! Don't think you've got any? Ask something anyway. Always have at least 2 questions such as: "Would you like daily email updates on progress, or would an update a few days out from the deadline work?" or "Will you or someone else be available via Skype should I have questions during the project?" and "Skype chat is a great way to communicate and get immediate answers. Is this something you or your company would be willing to do during the project?"
6. Follow up - most likely, the client will let you know when they will be back in touch. But it doesn't hurt to shoot off an email 10 to 15 minutes following your interview to let them know how much you're looking forward to working with them. And should they have any further questions, you'd be happy to answer them. You can do this on Upwork to using their internal messaging system.

By following these tips, you ensure that you're in the top 10% of side hustlers who interview well and will more often than not land the gig.

Hello, successful new side hustle!

More on following up
If you don't get the job, it's important that you still follow up with the client, particularly if the interview went well and it was just a matter of your fees or availability.

I recommend following up with clients (where you don't land the gig) every 3 months. Just a quick email to check in and make sure all went well with the previous job and that you're available to help if needed is enough.

If you do get the job, it's even more imperative that you follow up. Particularly if you're looking for ongoing work from this client.

Follow up with them 3 months following completion of the gig. Let them know how much you enjoyed working with them and that you're available for similar work if needed.

After this initial 3-month period, you should aim to follow up with either type of client every 6/9/12 months. However, this depends on the relationship and reception received from the 3-month follow-up, so play this by ear.

Use a spreadsheet or project management tool like Trello or Freedcamp, to track your clients, so you know when you've contacted them, followed up, etc. It will stop any annoying emails going out when a client has indicated he or she doesn't want to hear from you again.

And that's okay. You only want to work with clients that appreciate you and recognize your skills.

Product Pages

For Product-Based Side Hustles

"There is no try. There is only do or do not." ~ Yoda

In this section, we're going to focus on how to best convert your browsing customers to buyers. Because if you don't get this right, no matter how many products you have on your site, all you'll get in response is ... crickets. (again, cue chirping noise!)

Aside from have a well setup website, you'll want to make sure that all your product pages (which are really sales pages) are optimized the right way.

Optimizing Product Pages

When setting up your product pages, whether on your own website or a shopping platform like Etsy or Shopify, you want to make sure that you're giving your products the best visibility they can get.

This means stepping back and putting your marketing hat on and doing a bit of research.

I know, I know, all you want to do is create, but if you don't do this part of the process, you'll never reach your target audience and you won't make any money.

I know which camp I'd rather be in...

Here's some tips on what you can do with your product pages to ensure your customers find them:

#1: Photos
Invest in some high-quality photos that portray your product in the best light.

You want great lighting and your product set up in a way that makes people want to buy.

If you have a smartphone with a decent camera, you just need to get some good lighting and backdrops sorted.

Check out the resource on the **Tips and Tools Guide Resources page** for details on how to set up your own lightbox studio.

#2: Title
Now, you might be tempted to name your product

something really cute and funky, which is totally fine, but you'll also need to think about what your customer might be typing into a search bar when looking for your product.

Do they know the name of your product? Probably not. So while you can have a cute name for your product, in the title, you also want to add a couple of keywords that your customer might be searching for.

For example, if you are a clutch purse designer, you might have named your latest clutch "The Daisy".

What's the bet that not one of your potential customers is going to be searching for "The Daisy"?

Instead, what your title might say is "Hand-made clutch purse: "The Daisy".

#3: Product Description
Similarly with your product description, you want to include more of the keywords that your customers might be searching for.

Below is an example of the product description for "The Daisy" clutch purse from the previous point:

The Daisy hand-made clutch purse features an easy-close dome button and inside zipper pocket to catch all your small, delicate items.

Made from natural materials, this clutch purse is ideal for many occasions.

If you're looking for an evening clutch, The Daisy fits right in with any little black dress.

Need a day clutch? The Daisy will brighten up any outfit with it's bright, bold colors.

If you're wondering what keywords I was targeting, here's a list of what I targeted:

- Clutch purse
- Hand-made clutch purse
- Evening clutch
- Day clutch

Hopefully this gives you an idea of what you should be aiming for.

#4: Call-to-action

As well as using keywords in your product title and

description, you also want to add a call-to-action within your product's sales page that encourages people to buy your product.

Obviously, there will be a "buy now" button, but you also want to add something like the following sentence, to your product description:

What are you waiting for? Grab The Daisy clutch purse now! Simply click or tap the "buy now" button to get started.

As human beings, we love to follow instructions, so don't leave your customer wondering what to do, add a clear call-to-action to help them make the right decision — to buy your product!

Now that you've got that covered, it's time to make sure that your pricing is spot-on for your products or services.

Pricing and Rates

Pricing Services

If your side hustle is a completely new skill, you want to offer your services at a low price for at least the first 3 to 5 clients.

After that, you should look to increase your rate with each new client. I used increments of $5 per each new client until I reached my hourly rate of $55.

However, I don't charge myself out at an hourly rate. I charge per project, but it helps to have an idea of what your hourly rate is so you can price projects using that as your base.

I figure out pricing as follows:
1. Estimate the number of hours the project will take to complete; for example, let's say it was 5 hours.
2. Depending on the level of difficulty, I'll add an extra 2 to 5-hour buffer. Let's say it was 'easy,' then I'd add 2 hours; mildly difficult, I'd add 3 to 4 hours and difficult, the full 5 hours.
3. I'll then add 10% on top of that.

Here's how this looks as a calculation:

Estimated # hours + buffer hours + 10% = project fee

Using the figures from above, this would look like:

> 5 hours (5 x $55) + 2 hours (2 x $55) + 10% = $423.50 project fee

Setting your fees can be a bit tricky to begin with, but if you stick to the formula above, you'll get the hang of it.

Product Pricing
If you've got a product instead, look at similar products in the market and price your's accordingly.

Look at similar items on Etsy, eBay, or Amazon to get an idea for pricing.

If you're going to be on Etsy, then you definitely want to focus your research there, because those people will be your direct competition.

Make sure you take into account the cost to manufacture or create the product and then also add a percentage on for profit margins.

Your profit margin will largely depend on the market, so it's about finding a sweet spot.

If you can highlight why your product is better than someone else's, aka, what's your unique point of difference, then it's a lot easier to price your product at a higher price.

Great customer service also doesn't go astray when it comes to selling products.

The saying, "kill them with kindness" is appropriate, no matter how annoying a customer might be.

Now that you've got your product or service pricing sorted, it's time to figure out how you're going to market your brand new side hustle.

In the next section, we're looking at how you can make the sale. Turn the page to get started.

Marketing 101

"Hustle until your haters ask if you're hiring!" ~ Steve Maraboli

It's all well and good creating a website, optimizing your social media profiles, and deciding on your side hustle business idea.

But all that is useless if you don't get your business out there.

We talked about how to target your audience and find your clients and customers in the previous step. Now it's time to take it a step further and market your business.

The success of your side hustle will largely rest on how many clients and customers you can bring into your business.

And that, my friend, all boils down to how well you market your business.

Now I know, I know, marketing sounds like too much effort. It's hard and you don't have a background in marketing, so how are you supposed to know what to do?

That's what this section is all about!

MARKETING TIPS FOR SIDE HUSTLERS

One thing I hated about having to market my side hustle was that I thought it was going to be a massive sales pitch.

Hands up if you hate marketing because it always feels salesy!

I understand. It can feel like marketing your new side hustle is like you're pitching all the time. At times, you might even feel like you're coming across like one of those annoying used car salesmen.

And it feels icky, right?

What I didn't know—and what I'm about to share with you here—is that you can market your side hustle using different types of marketing strategies. They won't make you feel icky, or like you're on a major pitch-fest to your friends.

The key thing to remember is this:

> *If you're always looking for the sale, then you're always going to sound salesy.*

So that's what we're going to avoid. Instead, we're going to focus on implementing effective marketing strategies that focus on the end user experience —

how it benefits them.

How to Market Your Business With Online Marketing Strategies

#1: Education

One of the easiest ways to market your business is by providing educational content to your target audience.

You can do this in several ways:

- Writing how-to blog posts
- Providing free training videos about your side hustle
- Recording educational podcast episodes

The focus is on providing value first.

The key here is to make sure you include a call-to-action in each of these mediums. This could be to join your email list via a free gift you're giving away.

This could be a 3-part video tutorial or a discount code for your product.

The focus isn't on selling your side hustle though. The focus is on your target audience and what will benefit them.

#2: Utilize Facebook Groups

I've already mentioned this before, but you should be joining Facebook Groups where your target audience is hanging out.

In most of these groups, there will be days where you can share your product or service (generally called "promo" days).

You can also share your blog posts inside these groups too, so it's kind of a double-whammy in terms of ROI (return on investment) on your effort.

You encourage people to click through to read your blog posts and then they get on your list.

You can then market to them :-)

You can also show your expertise inside these groups by helping to answer questions people have. And if you're smart (which I know you are), you'll be capturing these questions and using them to create more content for your audience.

#3: Join HARO (Help a Reporter Out)

If you've not heard of this service, you will be amazed at how awesome it is.

HARO is a great way to establish your expertise and get featured on a website or inside a publication for free.

It's the best form of free advertising for your side hustle.

Once you're signed up, you'll receive two emails a day outlining requests for different types of information.

If there is a topic that fits in with what your side hustle is about, then you can submit your answer or information.

If your answer is accepted, you'll get free PR for your side hustle.

Publications that use HARO include Huffington Post, Forbes, Entrepreneur etc.

You can check it all out here: https://

www.helpareporter.com/

#4: Brand Yourself
Now, don't freak out! Branding doesn't have to be hard or cost a lot of money.

What you do need to know is who you are or who you want to be when it comes to your side hustle.

Your goal with creating your brand is to differentiate yourself in the market so that your target audience recognizes and relates to you immediately.

I actually love the branding side of things. It's about choosing colors, fonts, logos and tag lines that instantly make you and your side hustle recognizable to your audience.

Once you've got these nailed, you can then add them to your website and any media you share on social media etc.

I personally love using Canva.com for creating branded images. They provide you with templates and you will find a lot of different options to help you decide on your own branding.

#5: Create a Marketing Calendar

Marketing doesn't have to be hard and one of the easiest ways to remove any issues with marketing is having a marketing calendar.

This should include all your upcoming blog posts, what promotions you've got planned for your side hustle over the next 90 days, plus anything else that's relevant.

Once you see what you're focusing on, it's a lot easier to decide what type of marketing efforts you'll need.

If you're writing a blog post a week, you might add to the marketing calendar several social media posts to promote that blog post over the next 90 days.

If you're releasing a free 3-part video series, you'd also add that to the marketing calendar and decide on how you'll promote it.

Similarly, if you're running a sale on your site, add that to the marketing calendar and figure out how you're going to get the word out.

Marketing your side hustle doesn't have to be hard, but it does need some forethought and planning.

"Failing to plan is planning to fail." ~ Benjamin Franklin

If you you're not consistent with sharing your side hustle and getting the word out there, then it will be very difficult to be successful.

You should now have a clear idea about how you can 'make the sale' in your side hustle business.

In the next chapter, we're going to talk about some of the things that you MUST have set up in your side hustle to ensure you get paid.

Turn the page to get started.

Step 4 - Action List

Remember, these checklists are here to ensure that you don't forget anything and that you follow the process. If you get stuck, circle back to the last step or back to the beginning and just start again.

:: Checklist

- Download the templates for pitches and proposals
- Review the templates and revise to suit your needs
- Create a draft cover letter that you can reuse over and over again
- Set up your product pages and optimize as needed
- Determine your initial rate or product price and what you want your ideal price to be
- Ensure you have Skype set up properly
- Start applying for jobs!
- Set up your follow up reminders (as needed)
- Decide on how you'll market your side hustle and create a marketing calendar to keep track of what you've got planned

STEP 5: CONTRACTS, TERMS & BIZ SETUP

Contracts 101

For Service-Based Side Hustles

"Always have a formal contract agreement in place when working with a client. Failure to do so can mean loss of income for YOU." ~ Lise Cartwright

No matter where you find clients, you need to ensure that there is some type of contract in place. This ensures that all parties concerned know exactly what's expected, what the deadlines are, and how payments will be made.

When I first started my side hustle of SEO consulting, I found my first client on Upwork. This client offered me $1000 for keyword research, an onsite audit, and competitor analysis. This was across 4 websites.

To say I was excited was an understatement! I was ecstatic— I thought that if I could continue to get clients like this, I could leave my 'normal' day job pretty quickly!

However, there were a few mistakes I made with this particular client:

1. I didn't check the client's credentials.
2. I never received a deadline.
3. I failed to confirm with the client HOW or when they would pay me.

Unfortunately for me, my biggest mistake of all was failing to check the client's credentials. On sites like Upwork or Freelancer, you have an added level of security with regards to payment... PROVIDED the client has been *payment verified*.

I'm sure you can guess that my client WAS NOT payment verified.

What this meant was that because the client hadn't bothered to add payment details, there was no way that Upwork could seek payment from the client, even though I had completed the work.

And no, I never saw a cent of the money owed to me — massive lesson learned and one that almost turned me off doing any side hustle.

The only reason I stuck to it is that I landed another client at the same time (for freelance writing), willing to pay the same amount of money, who WAS payment verified.

I got paid without a hitch for that client!

The bottom line is, when you're applying for gigs on outsourcing sites, you want to make sure that the client is payment verified.

You can see if a client is payment verified on Upwork when viewing the job. On the right-hand side, where the client information is, it should have a green circle with a '$' sign there. If it's grey, then they are not payment verified... walk away!

What's great about working with outsourcing sites is that once the client is payment verified, there are no issues with payment, PROVIDED the client is satisfied with your work. Always remember that.

If you find a client via a job board site and you're dealing with the client directly, then make sure you have a formal arrangement in place.

I know many part-time side hustlers who fail to do this when they start out, and it's one of the reasons they decide that side hustling isn't for them.

But, if they had treated the side hustle as a 'proper' business or job and implemented a contract right from the start, I'm confident that many of these same side hustlers would have continued to move forward.

Here's what you must do when working with clients directly:

1. Implement a formal agreement - you can have something drawn up by your lawyer, or your can use a service like www.ourdeal.com where a variety of contracts are provided to suit multiple needs. This is the service I use.
2. Make sure that deadlines are communicated and clarified immediately following your hire.
3. Confirm payment details. Aim for 30%-50% upfront and then the remaining amount on completion of the project. This is standard practice. You could also opt for milestone

payments, which are payments made at each step of the project, or deliverable that you meet. For ongoing clients, I generally waive this and instead set up a recurring monthly fee, which is the end goal.
4. Confirm everything via email, and ensure that the client confirms the details so that everyone is on the same page.

If you don't have the funds to pay for a lawyer or for <u>Ourdeal.com</u>, then a simple search on Google should provide some options. You want to search for "Independent Contractor Agreement." This is a generic agreement that suits most side hustle skills.

You'll find an example of one of these in the **Tips and Tools Resource Guide** that you can amend for your own use as well. If you're not sure about any of this, seek professional advice.

In the next section, I'm going to talk about setting up terms for those of you who have a product-based side hustle.

Terms 101

For Product-Based Side Hustles

No matter where you find your customers, you need to ensure that there is some form of formal wording on your website or the online shopping platform your using.

You need wording around things like how you'll handle returns (if returns are allowed), what happens if the goods are faulty, and what to do if they don't like the product once they receive it.

There are a number of ways that you can generate these types of terms and if you're working with a site like Shopify, they provide some templates for you to work with.

Similarly, if you're using Etsy, they have some blanket terms, but it makes sense to have your own as well.

Review similar stores to yours and ensure you have terms listed on your website.

Some of these pages might include:

- Shipping
- Returns
- Faulty goods
- Change of mind returns
- Terms of service (for an online website)
- Payment methods accepted

At a minimum, you should have information about returns and how you deal with faulty goods.

You want to keep your customer happy, not annoyed!

In the next section, I'm going to talk about managing payments and business setup. Both are important aspects to consider. Learn what payment processor you should use and whether you need a business structure or not.

Managing Payments

So you've got your contract or terms in place. Now you're wondering what the best options are for receiving payments. This is important, especially if you're going to be working with international clients more so than local ones.

There are many options available, but these have the highest success rates and the lowest fees:

1. <u>PayPal.com</u> - this is what I use although the fees can be costly. I just factor those into the project fee. It's the cost of doing business, and the fees are tax-deductible.
2. <u>Dwolla.com</u> - an alternative to PayPal (but only available in the US), has lower fees.
3. <u>Payoneer.com</u> - an complete alternative to PayPal, it provides you with a US bank account. You do get charged fees overtime money is loaded into your account, but it's a great option for those of us outside the US (myself included).
4. <u>Stripe.com</u> - Similar to PayPal, and more commonly used as a payment processor rather than a way to issue invoices. Available in most countries t hat PayPal is available.
5. Direct payment into your bank account - use for local business only.

I like PayPal because I can get a monthly download of all incomings and outgoings that I can then upload to my accounting program.

Now before you freak out, you don't have to stress too much about accounting until you're dealing with more than two clients or are getting a lot of sales for your product.

Initially you can invoice clients directly from within PayPal or Dwolla, or you could just set up an invoice using Word or a free service such as Invoiceomatic.io.

You'll find an invoice template included in the **Tips and Tools Resources** page.

If you'd like to know how to use the invoicing option in PayPal and Dwolla, check out the videos on the Tips and Tools page too.

Tracking Income & Expenses

Regardless of whether you decide to use an accounting program at this point or not, you should be tracking your income and expenses for your own reference. A simple spreadsheet can be set up to do this.

Use a Google Docs one or whatever you have available on your computer.

Set it up as follows:

- One spreadsheet to track your income (create a tab for each month)
- One spreadsheet to track your expenses (create a tab for each month)

You can find a Google Docs template on the **Tips and Tools Resources** page for your use.

Next, let's talk about business setup: do you need to do this, what's involved and at what point should you even consider it? Learn all of this in the next section.

Business Setup

While we're briefly talking about accounting practices, let's chat about business setup too.

Now I know you're thinking to yourself, "Why do I need to worry about this?" and in reality, you don't, initially anyway.

Here's when you need to think about proper business setup:

1. You're earning more than $1,000 per month on top of your 'normal' job
2. You've got more than 3 clients or over 50+ sales per month
3. Clients are asking for your registered business number

Regardless of where you're at, you DO need to set up the following for your side hustle right now:

1. PayPal (or alternative) account
2. Separate bank account (doesn't need to be in a business name, can still be under your name, just separate to your 'normal' bank account) - check with your local bank first about their policies, some banks in the UK won't allow you to do this unless it is set up as a business name.
3. A way to invoice a client
4. A way to track your business income and expenses (for claiming at tax time)

I've already touched on PayPal/Dwolla and two ways to invoice a client.

Setting up a separate bank account is straightforward.

Tracking your income and expenses can be tricky. In the previous section, I mentioned using a spreadsheet to track your income and expenses. This is fine to use right now.

When I first started, I had NO idea what my business income and expenses were. Everything came into the one bank account, and to say it was a bit of a mess is an understatement!

It wasn't until 6 months after I went full-time that I started to track everything. I did this through a cloud-based tool called Freshbooks.com. This costs $20 per month for up to 25 client profiles.

There is a similar, free service called Nutcache.com that allows you to invoice, track expenses and track time as well.

Nutcache is just as robust as Freshbooks, so if you want to set up your accounting practices right from day one, use Nutcache or Freshbooks, regardless of whether your side hustle is service or product based.

What about a logo?
This is completely optional. With services available like Fiverr.com, you can have a logo created for less than $10.

You can add your logo to your invoices and also to your email signature.

It's definitely worth setting this up, and if you only spend $5, it's easy to replace it at a later date if you decide to go with something different further down the track.

What about business structure?
I'm NOT a qualified accountant or tax professional. You should seek advice from a qualified professional, particularly if you have ongoing questions.

Make sure you are diligent. Know what your particular location's tax requirements are BEFORE you start earning over $1,000 per month outside of your job.

Now that we've got the legal stuff out of the way, you're probably wondering if you should set up some type of business structure for your business.

In the beginning, I don't see any reason why you'd need to go beyond identifying yourself as a sole trader. This allows you to still claim taxes as well as business expenses against your current employed and side hustle incomes.

You will declare all your earnings on a normal tax form, with the only difference being that you can now claim more against ALL your taxable income due to your side hustle business expenses.

I'd highly recommend that you seek the services of a qualified accountant to help you at tax time. Better still, have a conversation with one prior to jumping into your side hustle. Or you could be like me and worry about the details later! It depends on how risk adverse you are.

Do what feels right to you.

If you do decide that you'd like to step into your side hustle full-time, taking your side hustle to the next level, you can still operate as a sole trader, or you can choose to set up a more formal business structure.

This area is definitely something you should seek professional guidance on before you make any decisions.

Step 5 - Action List

Remember, these checklists are here to ensure that you don't forget anything and that you follow the process. If you get stuck, circle back to the last step or back to the beginning and just start again.

:: Checklist

- Ensure you have contracts in place when dealing direct with clients
- Always check that clients are payment verified if using sites like Upwork to find jobs
- Make sure you've got the right terms on your product-based website so customers know exactly how things work
- Determine how you're going to receive payments
- Track your income and expenses either with a spreadsheet or utilize one of the cloud-based solutions
- Determine whether you need to register a business entity or not
- Seek professional advice if you have any questions at all

In the next chapter, we're going to look at how you should manage your side hustle with your current job and life. Failure to do this well can result in a nasty mess, so you definitely want to make sure that you have some kind of structure in place. Turn the page to learn how to manage your time well.

STEP 6: MANAGING TIME

Time Management

"The best way of learning about anything is by doing." ~ Richard Branson

Right, now you've picked a side hustle, figured out where to find clients, how to optimize your online profiles and how to pitch clients or customers. Now you need to figure out how you're going to balance your side hustle with your day job and social/family life.

The bottom line is - your current day job is your main source of income (right now). You definitely don't want to do anything to jeopardize your earnings here, so you need to figure out a good system to ensure that you don't have any issues arising between your two 'jobs.'

I'm going to share with you what I do, and I'll also provide links to other options as well, so you can choose the best idea that suits you.

CALENDAR MANAGEMENT

At the very heart of my time management system is my trusty Google Calendar (calendar.google.com). It's set up so that it syncs across all my devices. My MacBook Air, iPhone and iPad all connect together, so I can immediately see what's happening, no matter where I am.

When I first started out, I assigned colors to each client (Resource: https://support.google.com/calendar/answer/37095?hl=en) and scheduled them into my Google Calendar. This is a great way to see where you're at. I used green to show my personal time and then used other colors to represent different clients or activities.

But this can get a little tricky once you start to have more than a few clients! After my first 8 months freelancing on the side, I started to use Google Calendar and Evernote to manage my client deadlines.

Google Calendar + Evernote
Here's how this could work for you:

1. Set up a new notebook in Evernote for each client.
2. Create an ongoing checklist (with due dates) for each client.
3. Sign up for a Zapier account (you'll need this to connect the two together.).

The only problem with using Evernote in this way is that there is no real way to view all your upcoming deadlines in a calendar format – yes you can sort by note title (provided you've set it up the right way), but it's not an overall solution.

It'd like to make a big shout out to Mike Hale for finding a solution for this problem! In a recent blog post, he talked about syncing Evernote and Google Calendars using a site called Zapier.com to connect all the pieces.

Zapier is similar to IFTTT.com (If This, Then That) but can delve a bit deeper than IFTTT can. Zapier uses "Zaps" to create links between two apps, just like IFTTT does, but Zapier allows you to use a new note to create the trigger, IFTTT does not.

By connecting the two via Zapier, I was able to create a Google Calendar that would meet the needs of an overall client management calendar tool. Each time I create a new note from my client calendar notebook, it creates a trigger in Google Calendar to create an event.

Tips for a Quick Setup:

1. Setup a new calendar in Google Calendar before connecting to Zapier. This will ensure that you don't have any issues when trying to sync if the calendar is already there. Make sure you assign a colour to this calendar so that you can quickly identify it from your other calendar entries – by doing this, you can also just view your client calendar entries only.
2. Make sure that your Evernote notebook is set up the right way as well. Ideally, you want the deadline date in the note title, otherwise this won't work as well.
3. Create tags and make sure that your notes are tagged appropriately. I use content type tags to identify which type of content is going to, ie, blog post, Facebook, Pinterest, Twitter, YouTube etc – these are the tags I assign.

This worked really well for me and allowed me to keep track of the type of content I was creating and allowed me to see a few weeks out, just what I needed to do to prepare to ensure that I stuck to my client deadlines.

It's important that you figure out which method works best for you early on. Things can quickly spiral out of control, particularly when you're working with clients on the other side of the world.

I'm no longer using this setup, because as I started to take on more clients, I needed an even more robust way to manage all of this. Turn the page to learn what I'm doing now and how you can apply it to your current situation.

Lise's Time Management

After 18 months of doing things that way (Google Calendar + Evernote + Zapier), I implemented an even better system and added two apps into the mix, Trello.com and Todoist.com.

#1: My Google calendar is split into 3 main blocks of time:

1. Morning Action Block

2. Mind & Body Refresh
3. Afternoon Action Block

Now while this won't necessarily work for you while you are still working a day job, you can split your spare time into similar blocks of work.

Here's how:

1. First, figure out how much time per week you want to spend on your side hustle. Remember, you need to spend 5 to 10 hours a week to make $1,000 per month.
2. Make a note of that time.
3. Next you'll want to work out how those hours are going to be split during the week. Will you work weekends, how often will you work during the week, do you need to factor in social events, time with the kids?
4. Note this information down; then split your week nights and weekends as shown below (example shown is based on 10 hours per week).

Note: adjust to suit your needs. This is just a sample calendar of someone balancing a day job with a side hustle.

Monday
6 p.m. - 7:30 p.m. Mind & Body Refresh (dinner, family catch-up, relax)
7:30 p.m. - 8:30 p.m. Focused Hour Action Block
8:30 p.m. - 10:30 p.m. Relax & Review To-Dos for next day

Tuesday
6 p.m. - 7:30 p.m. Mind & Body Refresh
7:30 p.m. - 8:30 p.m. Focused Hour Action Block
8:30 p.m. - 10:30 p.m. Relax, etc.

Wednesday
6 p.m. - 8 p.m. Mind & Body Refresh
8 p.m. - 9 p.m. Focused Hour Action Block
9 p.m. - 10 p.m. Relax, etc.

Thursday
6 p.m. - 7:30 p.m. Mind & Body Refresh
7:30 p.m. - 9:30 p.m. 2-Hour Action Block
9:30 p.m. - 10:30 p.m. Relax, etc.

Friday
No work

Saturday

8 a.m. – 9 a.m. Mind & Body Refresh (breakfast + exercise)
9 a.m. - 11:30 a.m. 2.5-Hour Action Block
11:30 a.m. + Relax, etc.

Sunday
9 a.m. – 10 a.m. Mind & Body Refresh
10 a.m. - 12:30 p.m. 2.5-Hour Action Block
12:30 p.m. + Relax, etc.

You can split this up however you want.

It's important that when you get home from your job during the week that you give yourself a good hour or so to just eat, workout, and recharge. Spend time with your loved ones.

Don't go straight into working your side hustle, or you'll only burn yourself out and wish you'd never picked up this book! Just kidding... but you get my point.

Only take on what you can easily fit in with the time you have. Five hours per week is manageable, particularly if you don't want to work on the weekends. Remember, it's your choice; you decide how many hours you want to give to your side hustle.

#2: Once my calendar is set up in these 3 parts, I use Todoist to focus on the tasks that need to be done on a particular day.

You can use Todoist as well, in both your side hustle and day job. What's great is that you can set up projects (read: clients) and assign tasks against a project. Then you can set up deadlines and notifications that you can color code as well.

I use Todoist for everything that I need to get done. If it's not in Todoist, it doesn't happen.

#3: To manage all my client projects, I use Trello to keep track of all the details.

You can also use Trello in your side hustle AND day job.

The best part about Trello is that it's free and it's visual. Think of it as your side hustle project management system.

Between these three tools, I never miss a deadline.

Check out the videos on the Tips and Tools Resources page to see how to use these apps together.

A word on deadlines: if you've followed my advice to date, you should have already set deadlines with your clients. Make sure that you always allow yourself a 24 to 48-hour buffer.

What do I mean by this? Give the client one deadline and hold yourself accountable to one that is 24 to 48 hours earlier than that deadline. By doing this you'll avoid other things, like your day job, disrupting your best-laid plans.

To see a full list of all the tools I use in my business, visit my blog's resources page here: www.hustleandgroove.com/resources.

You'll find out exactly what makes my business tick!

Step 6 - Action List

Remember, these checklists are here to ensure that you don't forget anything and that you follow the process. If you get stuck, circle back to the last step or back to the beginning and just start again.

:: Checklist

- Determine how you will manage your time - which method will you implement?
- Ensure your deadlines are 24-48 hours prior to the clients deadline
- Buy The Productive Person (available on Amazon) for more details about Lise's time management process
- Download the Trello client management template

Now that we've gotten through the six steps (and workbook), you might be wondering what you need to do next.

Turn the page to find out what your next move is and how you can hit the ground running right away and start making your first $1000 in just 30 days!

WHAT'S NEXT

Where to From Here?

"Have faith in yourself. Think yes, not no. Live life to the full. NEVER give up." ~ Richard Branson

Let's do a quick recap on what we've covered:

- ✓ We've looked at some options for your side hustle and chosen an idea or skill to run with
- ✓ We've looked at your online presence and figured out what you need to set up or tweak
- ✓ We've looked at different options for finding clients, including outsourcing sites and social media sites
- ✓ We've looked at what you should include in a proposal to a client and what to include in an email pitch
- ✓ We've discussed contracts and best practices around what you should do to ensure everyone is on the same page

- ✓ We've looked at how you would manage the accounting side of things, including receiving payments and issuing invoices
- ✓ We touched briefly on business setup
- ✓ Lastly, we've looked at how to best manage your time and balance your day job with your side hustle

Does that about cover everything? It's a lot of stuff to cover in the one place and in the one sitting, so make sure you understand each area before you move onto each step.

Use the checklist (you'll find this in the Tips and Tools Resources page inside your workbook to print off) which has everything you need to do to get yourself up and running. Go here: http://www.hustleandgroove.com/shbresources16.

Use it to follow along and check your progress with setting up your side hustle and to ensure you don't miss a key step along the way.

30-Day Plan

Earning an extra $1000 in 30 days is achievable, if you take action. If you don't take action, nothing will change and you definitely won't be in the green by $1000.

Remember, Learn, Do, Repeat. That's what successful people do - let's add your name to that list.

To help you even further, grab the **30-day plan** on how to ensure you earn that extra moola.

You'll find it in the **Tips & Tools Resources page** for printing off.

RESOURCES

More Help...

As you go through the process of setting up your side hustle, there are some resources you'll need to help you along the way.

I've mentioned a number throughout the book and there are also a lot listed on the Tips and Tools Resources Page here: http://www.hustleandgroove.com/shbresources16 - which you have lifetime access to.

But there are always new options, so I wanted to provide you with more resources to ensure that you set up your business in the right way, from the very start.

TRAINING
There are plenty of options outlined on the Tips and Tools page to get further training, but here are even more places you can go to get access to free and paid training, no matter what your side hustle gig turns out to be:

- <u>Coursera</u> - this site gives you access to world-wide courses, all for free
- <u>Udacity</u> - this site gives you access to tech-based courses
- <u>KelbyOne</u> - this site is for budding photographers!
- <u>University of the People</u> - get a degree, tuition free
- <u>NovoEd</u> - great site for a multitude of online courses
- <u>Alison</u> - site that gives you access to free courses, ranging from food and nutrition through to web development
- <u>iVersity</u> - this site offers free online courses from qualified professors from around the world
- <u>MindBites</u> - need to just refresh your skills? This site offers a variety of short courses ideal for those that need to update existing skills
- <u>WizIQ</u> - fairly new site with limited course options, but does cover things like project management and music if these are areas of interest
- <u>Khan Academy</u> - this site offers a variety of online courses, ranging from maths through to art history

Not an exhaustive list by any means, but definitely one to give you plenty of options, no matter what your side hustle is.

BUSINESS SETUP

In Chapter 5, I talk about business setup, and while you don't need to worry about this initially, I believe it's easier to set things up at the beginning, like tracking income and expenses, rather than trying to implement something further down the track.

Here's what I'd recommend you do when starting out:

1. Utilize a cloud-based accounting platform like Freshbooks (paid) or Nutcache (free). Both are great options and allow you to track income, expenses and invoice clients directly. You can also set both of these up to allow your clients to pay you via Paypal and Dwolla.
2. Setup a separate bank account to receive all your client payments into (whether direct or from Paypal, Dwolla etc). This doesn't need to be a business account, it should be

in your own personal name. A savings account would work well as you can earn interest on your balances.
3. Depending on your country, you may need a business tax number. For the USA, this is an EIN, for Australia, this is a ABN. Refer to your country's tax website to find out what you need to do.
4. Find an accountant or bookkeeper that understands your country tax regulations and set up business best practice's according to their recommendations.

As discussed already, you don't need to worry about setting up a formal company structure until you decide to go full-time with your side hustle, and even then, you don't need to do that until you reach a certain income threshold.

Again, your country's tax website will provide all the information you need as well as seeking advice from your accountant.

CUSTOMER SERVICE
If you're looking at your side hustle as a long term gig, then I'd recommend implementing some customer service type solutions to your side hustle

business.

What do I mean by this? Let me explain further...

If you look at my website www.hustleandgroove.com, you'll notice a few things happen as you move around the site:

- ✓ A 'bar' appears at the very top of the page offering free training
- ✓ A box appears as you scroll down the page, offering a free giveaway
- ✓ On the right hand side, there is a help tab for people to send me a direct message if they'er stuck

These are all to help people get the answers they are looking for.

As you set up your side hustle business, think about ways you can make your clients/customers' experiences easier and no-fuss.

Here are a few tools I use that you might like to include on your website (when you have one):

- SoHelpful.me - this allows people to

schedule free, 30-min calls with you to discuss what they are looking for. It's a great way to find clients and it's also a great way to vet clients too — not everyone that approaches you for work should automatically get access to your time — always remember that!
- <u>SumoMe</u> - this site provides you with a number of free and paid plugins that you can add to your Wordpress site to make the user experience better, such as the help tab and social media sharing.

PRIVATE FACEBOOK GROUP

I've set up a private Facebook Group solely for people who have purchased any of the Side Hustle series of books.

Here you can ask questions and learn from other's about what they are doing.

I'm very active in this group, so make sure you join to find out even more about kicking off your side hustle and making some extra income within the next 30 days.

If you'd like to see a list of the resources I regularly

use in my own business, you can check them out on my website: www.hustleandgroove.com/resources

~~~

Congratulations! You're now equipped to start making some money from your side hustle.

Complete the action steps at the end of each chapter (Steps 1-6), follow the 30-day plan, use the checklist to make sure you've got everything set up and get your side hustle happening.

Do all this and you should be kissing your normal job good-bye in a short 8-10 months like I did!

If you have any questions or would like to provide some feedback, I'd welcome an email from you. Just send it to lise@hustleandgroove.com and I'll respond within 24 hours.

Alternatively, join the private Facebook Group — you can find details about how to join on the Tips and Tools page or at the beginning of the book.

Leave your questions there and I'll answer them for all the community to share.

Now don't just sit there, follow the steps, print the Tips and Tools Guide documents off (http://www.hustleandgroove.com/shbresources16), take action and I'll see you on the other side!

Remember, do what you love...

"Instead of wondering when your next vacation (holiday) is, maybe you should set up a life you don't need to escape from." ~ Seth Godin

About the Author

Lise is an author, blogger and sometimes-freelance writer and a self-confessed shoe fanatic – she's obsessed. Just ask her husband!

She has been looking for the magic in life since she was first exposed to positive, happy thoughts at the tender age of one - thanks Mum and Dad!

Lise can regularly be found at local cafes, NOT drinking coffee, but the more sophisticated and magical beverage that is a *Chai Latte*. She's also a bit of a baller, building her self-publishing empire an a crazy rate (think 3 books in 2 months!).

If you're looking to connect with Lise, you can connect with her via email, lise@hustleandgroove.com

Her online home is located at www.hustleandroove.com

CAN YOU HELP?

If you liked this book and it was helpful to you, could you please leave a review on Amazon? Simply visit Amazon to leave your review!

As a huge THANK YOU for doing this, send me an email (lise@hustleandgroove.com) with a link to your VERIFIED review and you'll get *30 minutes with me on a Skype call* – you can ask me any burning questions you have about **starting your Side Hustle!**

More Books by the Author

OFS Guide Series
- Book 1: Outsourced Freelancing Success: Start a Successful Freelancing Business and Make Your First Dollar Online!
- Book 2: Outsourced Freelancing Success: How to Set Freelancing Rates and Get Paid What You're Worth!
- Book 3: Outsourced Freelancing Success: How to Use Client Contracts to Protect Your Freelancing Business
- Book 4: OFS Guide to Setting Up and Structuring your Freelancing Business the Right Way
- Book 5: OFS Guide to Finding Clients Fast - The Top 57 Freelancing Job Sites for Finding High Paying Clients Now
- Book 6: 101+ Tools and Apps to Help Run Your Successful Freelancing Business
- Book 7: 18 Ways to Grow Your Freelancing Business in 30 Days or Less

No Gym Needed Series
- Book 1: No Gym Needed: Quick & Simple Workouts for Gals on the Go
- Book 2: No Gym Needed: Quick & Simple

Workouts for Busy Guys

If you're not a fan of the gym and like to get your exercise done in 30 minutes or less - these books are right up your alley!

Side Hustle Series
- Book 1: Side Hustle Blueprint: How to Make an Extra $1000 in 30 Days Without Leaving Your Day Job
- Book 2: Side Hustle Blueprint: How to Make an Extra $1000 per month Writing eBooks!

You can find all of these books available on Amazon.

DON'T FORGET TO GRAB THIS!

As a massive thank you for investing in my book, I'd love to offer you instant access to the Hustle & Grove Secret Vault of goodies + the SHB Workbook. Both will help you achieve success faster in your side hustle!

Visit here to get started: http://www.hustleandgroove.com/shb-bonuses